KidLit-O Presents

Career As A Pilot
What They Do, How to Become One, and What the Future Holds!

Brian Rogers

KidLit-O Books
www.kidlito.com

BRIAN ROGERS

Table of Contents

ABOUT KIDCAPS

KidLit-O is an imprint of BookCaps™ that is just for kids! Each month BookCaps will be releasing several books in this exciting imprint. Visit are website or like us on Facebook to see more!

INTRODUCTION

Two pilots prepare their plane before a flight[1]

Have you ever had the chance to fly on an airplane? Maybe you were going to visit family or maybe you were going on a vacation with your family to a faraway place. Either way, do you remember how exciting it felt as the plane's

---

[1] Image source: http://tinyurl.com/n7mqr8n

engines roared to life and as you sped down the runway, gathering speed until the wind finally was forced beneath the plane's wings and you were lifted into the air? Were you worried that the plane would crash or fall back down to the earth? Did anyone around you look afraid?

A little over 100 years ago, flying was something that people could only dream of. It was only when brothers Orville and Wilbur Wright successfully flew their homemade airplane for about 120 feet in 1903 that people around the world could begin to seriously think about what it would be like to be a pilot. Nowadays, the situation is much different. Thousands of planes take off and land all around the world every day, and millions of people in hundreds of countries have had the opportunity to travel long distances in relatively short times, thanks to the miracle of powered flight. Instead of spending long weeks on ocean voyages or countless months crossing the country in covered wagons, business people and tourists alike can now fly to the other side of the world for a meeting and still be home in time for dinner.

But all of these planes don't travel around the world by themselves. Each one of them needs a pilot, someone to fly the aircraft. Have you ever thought about what it would be like to be that pilot and to be in control of a huge passenger plane as it cruises from one side of the country to the other? Have you ever imagined how it would feel to travel at extremely high speeds and to visit many different cities around the world?

In this handbook, we will be taking a close look to see what having the career of a pilot involves. Although there are all types of pilots in the skies, we will be focusing mainly on airline pilots - the men and women who fly large airplanes full of ticketed passengers. What would you like to know about being a pilot?

We will look at the career of an airline pilot from seven different angles in seven different sections. In the first section, we will talk about what a pilot does and what different kinds of pilots are working today. We will see a little bit of what a pilot's work schedule is like and what kind of money a pilot can expect to make, both at the beginning and towards the end of their career.

The second section will tell us what the training is like to become a pilot. As you can imagine, a pilot has a lot of responsibility on their shoulders. After all, he or she is in charge of a multi-million dollar aircraft and all the lives of the people sitting inside it. Can you imagine how much training is needed to make sure that the pilot is well-qualified for the job? As you will see, the path to becoming an airline pilot can take many years and involves receiving a detailed education from qualified instructors both on the ground and in the air.

The third section will answer the question: "Is being a pilot an easy job?" As you can probably imagine, the answer to that question is a definite "no". Being a pilot can actually be a stressful job day in and day out, and in this section we will examine all that is required of a pilot. Did you know that pilots are expected to be experts in many areas, including science, engineering, and legal matters? We will see what makes the job of a pilot so demanding and what some of the unique challenges that come with it are.

The fourth section will show us what the average day is like for an airline pilot while they are at work. Unlike other jobs that have a set time to start and set time to go home, being a pilot means working at all kinds of strange hours often for long stretches of time. We will learn what a pilot can expect to do during an average day at work and what kinds of experiences he or she may have.

The fifth section will tell us about some of the difficult moments of being a pilot that arise every now and then that make some people decide that being a pilot is not the career for them. What are these difficult circumstances and how do successful pilots deal with them? We will find out in the fifth section.

Then the sixth section will tell us a little about what the future holds for pilots. In ten years or so, right about the time that you may decide whether or not being a pilot is the right career for you, do you think that there will there be a lot of jobs available? Will pilots fly to new destinations or even use different types of aircraft?

Finally, the seventh section will tell you what you can do right now to get ready to become a pilot. Although most airline pilots need to have a college education before they can get a job flying professionally, there are certain qualities and skills that you can develop right now to help you reach your goals more quickly. Even while you are still living at home and going to school, you can start to think and act like an airline pilot, even going so far as to get your pilot's license.

Being an airline pilot is an exciting and often glamorous job. Pilots get to look down the world from high above, travel to exotic places, and receive the respect of lots of people. While their job can be tough at times, there are certainly many experiences that they couldn't have if they had chosen any other career. Are you ready to learn more about this exciting job and to decide whether or not it's for you? Then let's get started with the first section.

CHAPTER 1: WHAT DOES AN AIRLINE PILOT DO?

Airline pilots are in charge of safely getting planes from one place to another[2]

---

[2] Image source: http://www.bls.gov/ooh/transportation-and-material-moving/airline-and-commercial-pilots.htm

Simply put, a pilot is the person in charge of flying a plane. If there are other people on the plane with them, like a co-pilot, a navigator, or several flight attendants, then the pilot is the one in charge of making sure that each person on the flight crew knows exactly what is expected of them and that any problems that come up are resolved quickly and safely. While this handbook will be talking mainly about airline pilots, let's take a moment to talk about what other kinds of pilots are out there flying in the skies of the world.

First, there are private pilots. These are pilots who fly smaller planes, powered both by propellers and by jet engines. A private pilot may fly for recreation or to get to and from work in certain isolated areas, and they may even take one or two people along for the ride. Some private pilots may be quite wealthy, although not all of them own their own planes. Some rent planes and others share a plane with a flying club and take turns using it throughout the year.

There are other pilots who fly aircraft other than planes. Some fly helicopters, hot air balloons, and vehicles called sailplanes. These pilots may carry passengers around to see beautiful areas from above while others work for news stations recording news events and traffic from above.

Then there are pilots who fly large planes which, while they don't carry any passengers, are filled with all kinds of momentous packages including mail, presents, books, TVs, and even emergency supplies for people who are suffering. These cargo pilots fly all over the world, and everyone is always terribly excited to see them. Have you even gotten a package in the mail? That package may have been sent to you using an airplane.

In the military, there are pilots who fly cargo planes and others who fly combat aircraft. For example, some military pilots fly planes that can drop lots of bombs on targets far below them while other pilots fly jets and helicopters designed to fight against small targets and enemy aircraft. Other trained military pilots never even leave the ground and instead fly "drones", or aircraft that don't need pilots, to faraway targets.

There are also experienced pilots, both inside and outside of the military, who share their experience and work as flight instructors helping new pilots learn how to fly.

But this handbook is focused on the type of pilots that we see terribly often - airline pilots. On most planes, there are at least two pilots, who are called the Captain and the First Officer. On some other airplanes, there may even be a third pilot in the cockpit called the Second Officer. Although the Captain is the one in charge of the airplane, the First and Second Officers can help the Captain in case of an emergency and can take over flying duties on extremely long flights. Each pilot has a radio headset so that they can communicate clearly with the rest of the crew. Once the plane takes off, the pilots lock themselves in the cockpit so that no hijackers or terrorists can get inside and take over the plane.

The average pilot may work anywhere from eight to twenty days per month. Does that sound good to you? Well, when you think that most people must work at least twenty days per month, it seems like pilots actually have it kind of easy. Despite appearances, pilots have to work extraordinarily long hours. How does that happen?

Pilots in most areas actually end up spending up to 100 hours in the air per one month and are allowed to fly a maximum of 900 hours per year. But for a flight of three hours, the pilot may spend much longer examining which route to take, making sure the plane is safe to fly, filling out paperwork, and waiting for permission to take off from and land at different airports. So although a pilot may only spend 100 hours flying per month, they may end up spending much more time than that working in other aspects of their job.

How much money can an airline pilot expect to make? Well, a lot depends on how much experience the pilot has and what their official position is (Captain, First Officer, etc.). In most areas, a new airline pilot will begin as either a Second or First Officer, depending on how many pilots are assigned to each plane in the airline. New pilots can hope to make at least $20,000 to $50,000 per year. While that may be enough money to support a family in some areas, $50,000 per year probably won't make anyone a millionaire. But new pilots know that they are also paid in experience. What does that mean?

Pilots don't calculate their experience like other types of careers - counting months or years on the job. When pilots measure their experience they talk about "flight hours", or how many hours they have spent in the air in control of an aircraft. While a new pilot may not make a lot of money in the beginning, especially when compared with other careers, a pilot knows that their first few years on the job are immensely valuable because they gain experience that will eventually help them get a better position (and more money).

After a Second Officer has gained a lot of experience, they can be promoted to First Officer, who sits to the right of the Captain and helps him or her to fly the plane. After a First Officer has gained a lot of experience and spent many hours in the air, they can be promoted to Captain. How much money does a Captain expect to make? While the actual number may be a little different for each airline, most Captains can expect to make $165,000 or more per year.

Pilots work together as a team to make sure that the plane arrives safely at the correct destination each and every time that it takes off. While they may not make as much money as doctors or lawyers, pilots love their jobs and love spending their days in the air looking down on the world.

What is the training like to become an airline pilot?

At ground school, future pilots learn the science of flight[3]

---

[3] Image source: http://ascendaviationllc.com/private-pilot-ground-school/

A pilot has to understand what makes a plane fly, how to fix basic mechanical problems, and what to do in case of an emergency. Pilots can do all this because they receive excellent training and put into practice everything that they learn. So what kind of training does an airline pilot receive? Each future airline pilot receives two types of training: training on the ground and training in the air. Let's have a look at each of these types of training to see what all airline pilots must learn before they can get a job with a major airline.

The first step for most pilots is to get a Bachelor's Degree after studying for four years at a local college. Although the exact subject that they study isn't hugely important, airlines will be interested to see that a pilot knows how to set a goal and not to give up until they reach it. Airlines are looking for people who are hard workers and who don't run away when they meet with a challenge. Some future pilots choose to study for a Bachelor's in Science degree with a special focus on aviation (flying), but it is not necessarily the only acceptable subject to study.

Once a future airline pilot has graduated from college and has obtained a four year degree, it is time for them to learn the specific things that a pilot needs to know. Before they actually get behind the controls of an airplane and take flying classes, many experts recommend that the future pilot go through something called "ground school". What is "ground school"? Ground school is a series of classes that teach the future pilot about the physics of flying, how to use a plane's instruments, how to navigate, how airplanes are maintained and fixed, and how different kinds of weather affect flight. For some people, learning all this would be pretty boring and they may be impatient to just get up in the air and fly. But why do you think that many experts say that future pilots should go to ground school first?

Ground schools (which are usually found at local airports) teach pilots the basics of flying. The fact is that flying is devilishly difficult, and a pilot must always be making calculations in their head, looking at their instruments, and thinking about possible problems and how to avoid them. If a student thinks that learning the basics of flying is boring while at ground school, chances are that person will not know how to handle an emergency in the future. Why not? Because they did not take the time to study the science of flight, which means they may do something dangerous and make a bad situation even worse. So if a new student is bored during ground school and doesn't want to learn about how to handle different problems that an airplane may have, then that person probably shouldn't spend the time and money to learn how to fly because they most likely won't make a decent pilot.

Once a future pilot has completed ground school, they will want to begin flight school. Flight school uses simulators and actual air-planes to teach pilots how to fly under all sorts of circumstances, including bad weather and complete darkness. The advantage of using a simulator (which kind of looks like a big video game) is that any mistakes the pilot makes don't end up destroying the airplane or hurting any passengers. Later on, a new pilot will go up in their airplane with an instructor sitting right next to them, just like a student learning to drive a car. The instructor will be ready to take over or to help the pilot out in case of an emergency.

When with their instructor, pilots must learn how to get control of the plane in case the engines stop or the plane starts to fall. In fact, if you go to your local airport, you might be able to see new pilots turning off their engines on purpose and learning how to stay calm keep control of the plane. Pilots also learn how to fly using only on the different gauges and instruments that are in the dash in front of them, useful when they can't see outside the windows. In flight school, pilots learn how to handle emergencies and they get to count the hours that they spend in the air. After all, it is the flight hours that count. Before they can get their Private Pilot Certificate (PPC) and fly a plane by themselves, a pilot needs to have spent at least 40 to 60 hours up in the air, learning how to handle an airplane. The cost for ground school and flight lessons may cost the pilot anywhere from $10,000 to $12,000! Do you see why some people have to think seriously carefully before they start training to become a pilot?

After the pilot has learned the basics of flying and can fly a small aircraft by themselves, the time has come for them to get more serious about their career and to start filling the requirements to become a professional pilot. The next step for many pilots is to pass a special medical examination carried out by a doctor working for the Federal Aviation Administration (FAA), which is the governmental organization that makes sure that American skies are kept safe and that only qualified pilots can fly in them. The medical exam will make sure that the pilot's vision (even if he or she uses glasses) is good enough to let them fly and that the pilot doesn't have any problems with drugs or alcohol.

After getting their PPC and passing the FAA medical exam, a private pilot will want to prove that they have the knowledge and skills to be paid to fly. In other words, they will need to get their Commercial Pilot License (CPL). This license will allow the pilot to fly larger planes and to get paid for their work. Along with having to learn about the specific plane that they will be flying, a pilot needs to get something called an "Instrument Rating", a combination of a written test and a flight with an instructor that will show that a pilot understands advanced flight concepts and that they can fly their plane using only the instruments in case of low visibility or some kind of other unusual condition. To get a CPL, a pilot must have at least 250 hours of flying experience. For 100 of those hours, the pilot must be in a position called the "Pilot in Command", which means that they are actually the person in charge. 50 of those hours must be spent on longer cross country flights, and at least 10 of those hours flying with an instructor, especially in the case of more complex aircraft. Some new pilots actually try to get work as a flight instructor so they can get valuable flight experience and get paid for it!

After they have their Commercial Pilot License, a pilot will try to gain even more experience (and keep doing what they love) by getting a job flying some sort of aircraft. They may get work with a delivery company like UPS or FedEx, or they may get a job for a private company carrying employees and cargo from one place to another. Even though commercial pilots earn less money than airline pilots do, commercial pilots are happy to be up in the air and behind the controls of any sort of aircraft. Some commercial pilots hope to gain enough experience to be able to apply later on for a position with an airline.

From time to time, an airline will announce that they are looking for more pilots. How can a pilot qualify for a job with an airline? They must become an ATP (Airline Transport Pilot) by taking a devilishly difficult written test and show proof that they have gained over 1,500 hours of flight experience. Airlines may hire one or two hundred pilots all at once, and other times they will look for just a few at a time. The competition may be very high – perhaps with thousands of qualified pilots all trying to get the same few jobs.

For those who are hired, they will spend the next few weeks getting specialized training for their new job, which will likely involve one week learning about the airline itself and anywhere from three to six weeks going to a specialized ground school and working with a simulator. The airline will require that all of their new pilots have at least 25 hours of flying experience with the planes they will be flying and the pilot will have to prove their abilities by completing a flight with an FAA agent sitting next to them and watching their every move!

After their initial training, the new pilot will begin either as a Second or First Officer and will be put into a rotation of flights. With time, they can hope to be promoted to Captain and to get better routes and more money. Captains will have to pass a medical exam twice per year to make sure that they are in top physical shape, and most other pilots will have to pass a medical exam one per year.

Some other folks may choose a different route than the one that we have considered - receiving training from the military to become a pilot. Whether it is with the Coast Guard, the Air Force, or the Navy, a person can serve their country for ten years or more and in exchange will be trained and become qualified for almost any flying job that they may apply for later on. While signing up with the military may be a good option for some people, it may not be great for others. For example, some people may not feel comfortable flying in combat or spending so much time away from their families in times of war. Each person should carefully weigh the costs and benefits of military training before making a decision.

CHAPTER 2: IS BEING AN AIRLINE PILOT AN EASY JOB?

Do pilots spend all their time relaxing on the job?[4]

After seeing all of the training that a pilot must receive before they can begin flying professionally, you would probably agree that the road to becoming a pilot is not an easy one to travel. In fact, some experts say that 80% of those who begin training to become pilots never even get as far as qualifying for their Private Pilot Certificate! But once a professional pilot has gotten a job with an airline, does that mean that the hard work is all over with and that they can just sit back and take it easy? After all, modern planes have computers to help the pilots fly the plane and to get to their destinations safely. So it can't be that hard, right?

Let's have a look at everything that a pilot is expected to know and to constantly think about as they fly through the air and then you can decide for yourself whether or not being an airline pilot is an easy job.

First off, an airline pilot is expected to understand the **physics of flying**. What does that

---

[4] Image source: http://ranchogramma.blogspot.com/2011/02/is-for.html

mean? Well, as you probably know, flying is all about getting enough speed on the ground so that the air goes under the wings of the plane and actually lifts it up into the sky. How fast does each type of plane need to travel to stay in the air? How sharp can a plane turn before it loses too much speed and starts to fall? At what angle does the plane need to land in order to safely get the passengers onto the ground? This is the type of information that each pilot needs to know in order to do their job. Can you imagine what would happen if a pilot tried to slow down their airplane in mid-air too much and accidentally made it fall out of the sky?

An airline pilot also needs to understand how different types of **weather** affect flight. For example, way up in the sky, the weather is often much different than it is on the ground. What happens if a plane gets ice on its wings? Does a jet engine do better in cold weather than a propeller engine? What should a pilot do if large hailstones start to fall while they are flying? A good pilot knows how weather forecasts will affect their trip, and they know what kinds of weather are dangerous and how to react to each individual situation.

Airlines pilots also need to understand the basics of **maintenance** and the **mechanics** of their aircraft. Why is it so important that pilots understand how their plane works and how to take care of it? When they are up in the air, sometimes planes have problems, just like cars on the road sometimes break down and need to be fixed. Pieces on an airplane may break, wires may burn, and instruments may stop working. A pilot knows that the mechanic will not be up in the air with them, so they must be prepared themselves to fix any pieces that may break and to safely resolve any problems. Pilots must also understand how their plane is built and how it works, to thus avoid making the plane do something that it is not meant to do - like turning too sharply, going too high, or landing on a runway that is too short or not able handle the plane's weight.

Airline pilots also need to understand everything about **navigation** - how to know where they are at all times and how to get to their destination. Early pilots used to just fly low above the ground, using roads and mountains to guide them. Later on, pilots used tools like compasses and maps to guide themselves.

Modern pilots use satellites and sophisticated radar systems to across the globe. While modern tools help a pilot to make sure of where they are, what do you think would happen if the Global Positioning Satellites (GPS) that a pilot uses stopped working? Or what would happen if the radar on the ground lost power? A pilot needs to know how to get to where they are going even if all of their technology fails. They can use charts, the radio, and even their eyes to get where they are going in case of instrument failure.

In certain situations, a pilot may need to make an emergency landing at the nearest airport. But is every airport okay to land at? The answer depends on politics and on **current events**, something that pilots need to keep up to date on. A pilot needs to know if certain parts of the world are dangerous, who the friends of their country are, and what places aren't safe to fly over. In the next section, we will learn about the tragedy of Korean Air Lines Flight 007, where the pilots were not aware that they were flying over the territory of an enemy nation and their mistake resulted in lots of death and destruction.

Pilots must learn from all such **past accidents**. They try to learn what went wrong, what mistakes were made and what unsafe conditions were allowed to develop so that something similar never happens again. While it may be sad to have to sit down and read about people who died in plane accidents and the scary things that happened to them, the lessons that future pilots can learn will save many lives and help to avoid senseless tragedies.

Pilots must also obey **flying regulations**, know the limits of **radio and radar technology**, and recognize certain symptoms of **flight sickness** in their crew and passengers.

After seeing all that is expected of a pilot from day to day, do you think that being a pilot is an easy job? You would probably agree that being a pilot is actually a hugely demanding career that requires the best efforts of the people involved each and every time that they climb into the cockpit to fly.

CHAPTER 3: WHAT IS AN AVERAGE DAY LIKE FOR AN AIRLINE PILOT?

A pilot going over a pre-flight checklist[5]

---

[5] Image source: http://0to30in60.com/one-day-before-day-1-final-checklist/

An airline pilot works on a rotating schedule, which means that the days and times that they work are different each week. Once they receive their schedule a pilot will make sure that they are at the local airport (where they are "based out of") in plenty of time for the flight. The planes belong to the airline and are often parked either at or near the gate from one night to the next.

Once they arrive at the airport, pilots pass through security like everyone else and then head towards the airplane. Pilots and other crew members are the first ones on the plane. While the mechanics give the aircraft necessary maintenance and fill the tanks up with fuel, the pilots will go through a long checklist to make sure that important instruments are working and that they know exactly which route they will take to arrive at their destination. The Captain will take his or her seat on the left, the Copilot (or First Officer) on the right, and on some planes a Flight Engineer (or Second Officer) will sit in a third seat behind the Co-Pilot.

After going through the long and detailed pre-flight checklist, the Captain will check with the flight attendants to make sure that all the passengers are seated and then the control tower (which is filled with Air Traffic Controllers) will tell the pilots when they can leave and which runway they should use. This is important, because you can imagine what a disaster it would be if two planes tried to use the same runway at the same time, or if one plane landed on the runway as another was trying to take off.

Once the crew receives permission to take off, the pilots will go to the runway and increase the speed, adjusting the wings so that the wind pushes the aircraft up into the air. Once the plane is in the air, the control tower will tell the pilots what altitude they should fly at so that they don't accidentally crash into another plane. A special set of flight rules (called Visual Flight Rules, or VFR) says that pilots headed in certain directions must fly at certain altitudes. Pilots who obey these rules make sure that no midair collisions ever happen.

Whether on a short or a long flight, the pilots will use their instruments to make sure the plane is level, going the right speed, going in the right direction and that it avoids any obstacles like mountains or dangerous weather systems. They will inform the local control tower of any problems and will constantly check their position and make sure that each part of the plane is working correctly. Once they reach their destination, good communication with the tower will make sure that they land on the correct runway and then they can taxi (move on the ground) to the correct gate to drop off their passengers.

After the passengers have left the plane, the pilots will perform a few more checks and make sure that the plane doesn't have any problems after the flight, which may have lasted anywhere from a few hours to ten or more, depending on the final destination. Then the pilots will get off the plane and go rest for a while before taking another flight back to their home base, where they will most likely get several days off. Some pilots, even though they aren't officially assigned to work, will have to remain "on call", which means that, at any moment, they might get a phone call telling them to go to work.

CHAPTER 4: WHAT IS THE HARDEST PART OF BEING AN AIRLINE PILOT?

Captain Sully and the plane he landed on the Hudson River[6]

Being an airline pilot can be a hugely challenging yet rewarding career choice for lots of young men and women. But as you can probably imagine, being a pilot also means having lots of very intense moments that make some people think that this is not the career for them. What are some of these very specific challenges and how do pilots deals with them? Let's look at three hard parts of being an airline pilot to learn the answer.

Seniority: Do you know what the word "seniority" means? It refers to the amount of time that a person has been doing their job. In most airlines, salaries are raised for, promotions are given to, and the best routes are chosen by the pilots with the most seniority. That means that even if you are the best pilot in the company, there is no guarantee that you will make more money, get better routes, or get promoted if there is someone else who has been with the company longer than you. Can you understand why some pilots feel kind of frustrated with

---

[6] Image source:
http://www.people.com/people/article/0,,20309348,00.html

their jobs, knowing that they can't advance in their careers until some of the older pilots quit or retire?

Pilots have accepted that seniority is not going away, so they try to work hard and build up a good reputation at their company so that they don't get fired. That way, they know eventually they will get a promotion and a raise.

No guarantee of job security: In most jobs, you can feel secure knowing that once you are hired you will have a place to work for the rest of your life. In the world of airlines, however, there are no such guarantees. Airlines may merge (combine) with other companies or they may even go entirely out of business. Can you imagine getting a phone call one day telling you that you no longer have a job? Or worse yet, can you imagine hearing about it on the news?

What happens to a pilot's seniority when they change from one company to another? In most cases, what counts is not the time that a person has been flying but how long they have been with a certain airline. So even if a pilot has been flying for twenty years, if their airline goes out of business and forces them to look for a new job that pilot must start all over again from the bottom, most likely as a Second Officer. Can you imagine how hard it would be to go from working as a Captain to a Second Officer?

Pilots have learned not to worry about the things that they can't control. Like weather and politics, the economy may affect the job of a pilot, and the best thing that a pilot can do is react well to the situation.

Responsible for the lives of others: Depending on the size of the aircraft, a pilot may be responsible for the lives of anywhere from a few dozen to a few hundred passengers. If the pilot makes a bad decision or doesn't react well to a certain situation, then all of those lives on the plane will be affected, and people may even end up dying. Can you imagine having so much responsibility put on your shoulders each and every time that you go to work?

Flying conditions can be unpredictable from one day to the next. A routine flight can become dangerous if a storm system moves into the path of the flight, if a mechanical problem affects one of the engines or the landing gear, or if a passenger tries to cause a problem. The way that pilots react to these unpredictable changes can often mean the difference between life and death. Would you like to see some examples of good and bad behavior by pilots? Let's examine three examples:

GOOD EXAMPLE: On January 15, 2009, Captain Chesley Sullenberger took off from La Guardia airport in New York City headed for North Carolina. But about three minutes into the flight the plane flew through a flock of geese and some of the birds got sucked into the plane's engines. Both engines were damaged and stopped working. The plane began to fall out of the sky. Over his radio, Captain Sullenberger discussed different options with the air traffic controller, but finally decided to "ditch" (crash on purpose) the plane into the Hudson River near some boats. The plane had a safe landing, all of the passengers were evacuated and rescued by the boats, and Captain Sullenberger was the last person to leave the plane. None of the passengers or crew members died, thanks to the Captain's excellent flying.

BAD EXAMPLE: On November 12, 2001, a routine flight from JFK airport in New York City to the Dominican Republic turned deadly when it crashed into a Queens neighborhood just a few minutes after takeoff. Although some people were worried that terrorists may have been involved, it was soon discovered that the First Officer (along with some slight mechanical problems) had led to the crash. What happened? An earlier plane had made the air a little bumpy. The First Officer panicked when his plane began to bounce and overreacted, swinging the tail rudder from side to side trying to stop the bouncing. The tail rudder broke from all the actions of the First Officer and the plane soon spun out of control and crashed, killing 265 people. Although some experts feel that the rudder could have been designed to hold up better under extreme force, it was also shown that the First Officer could have prevented the crash by not overreacting and making so many adjustments to the tail rudder.

BAD EXAMPLE: On September 1, 1983, Korean Air Lines Flight 007 disappeared in the Sea of Japan, and all 269 people on board were declared dead. The plane had taken off from Anchorage, Alaska, and was en route to Seoul,

South Korea. When the plane disappeared, it was about 300 miles off course. What had happened? After a thorough investigation, it was learned that the autopilot had been set incorrectly and that the pilots were not paying attention to the instruments that would have told them that they were getting further and further off course. Eventually, the plane flew over the USSR, which at the time was an enemy of the United States. The USSR thought that the plane was a spy plane, and so they shot it down. By not paying attention to their instruments and not using the autopilot correctly, the pilots of KAL 007 were directly responsible for taking the passengers into a dangerous situation that led to everyone on board losing their lives.

Not everyone can deal with the rules of seniority, the lack of job security, and the responsibility over the lives of others that come with being a pilot. Anyone who is seriously considering the career of an airline pilot should understand the stress that comes with the job and make sure that they are ready to handle it.

CHAPTER 5: WHAT DOES THE FUTURE HOLD FOR AIRLINE PILOTS?

In ten years or so, maybe around the time that you may decide to pursue the career of an airline pilot, will there still be lots of jobs? Will any new types of jobs be available for pilots in the future? Before we get started, it would be a brilliant idea to see what one truly experienced instructor had to say about the airline industry. He said: "The future in aviation is the next 30 seconds -- long-term planning is an hour and a half."[7] What did the instructor mean with those words? He meant to say that so many

---

[7] Quotation source:
http://science.howstuffworks.com/transport/flight/modern/pilot2.htm

things about flying can change so quickly that it can hard to predict what the future will hold. Politics, the economy, and even wars can affect how many pilots have jobs and where airlines can and cannot fly to. Even though no one can say for sure what the world of flight will be like in ten years, there are some seriously smart people who have come up with some interesting ideas. Let's see at what they are saying.

Fewer airlines: Since 2005, the nine major airlines in the United States have merged (combined) to form just five major airlines. While the actual number of flights may not have changed too much, it does mean the passengers who want to fly have fewer options to choose from and that pilots looking for jobs have fewer airlines to apply for. Ticket prices have actually gone up, which may lead to fewer passengers being able to afford to fly, some people think that it may actually end up hurting the airline industry and causing some airlines to have to close their doors, which in turn may lead to even fewer flights, and even higher ticket prices.

Pilots may go into space: As technology gets better and better, private companies like Virgin

Galactic are planning to take everyday passengers (and not only trained astronauts) into space for short flights, where they can spend several minutes in complete weightlessness. What does this mean for pilots? Well, think about it- someone will have to fly those spacecraft! In the future, it is possible that more and more pilots will be able to find jobs flying in outer space and not just from one city to another.

Planes may look majorly different: Today, planes look at lot like buses with wings. But in the future, new technology may change the way that planes look. Instead of carrying just one row of passengers (with the cargo placed below them) planes may be able to carry way more people and cargo. How would that be possible? The "Clip-Air" project out of a technology school in Switzerland may have come up with a new design for planes to make them more efficient. Each plane could carry one or more long containers that could be transported on railroad tracks, which would make them easier to load and unload. This way, more people could be carried with each flight and less time would be wasted loading and unloading each plane. Can you imagine seeing these strange looking planes flying through the skies?

The new Clip-Air technology could change the way that planes are made[8]

In the future, the world will still need pilots. While there are no guarantees on how many airline pilots will be needed, you can be sure that space travel and other new ideas will create future jobs that we can't even imagine yet.

---

[8] Image source: http://tinyurl.com/mwxf3yv

CHAPTER 6: HOW CAN I GET READY NOW TO BECOME AN AIRLINE PILOT?

This young British girl, named Sally Cluley, became a pilot when she was only 16 years old[9]

Even though airlines require that a pilot be at least 18 years old before applying for a job (and most airlines also like to see a college degree), there are several skills and abilities that you can work hard to develop right now that will help you stay on the path to becoming an airline pilot. Let's have a look.

First, you should develop math and science skills. A good pilot knows how to make complex calculations in their head to be able to determine how fast they need to travel, what direction they should take to reach their destination, and how best to react in an emergency. As we saw earlier, ground school shows pilots how the math and science they learned in college will lift their plane into the air and keep the passengers safe. So study hard to be able to work well with both of these subjects.

Second, learn how to be a good communicator. Do you remember the exciting story of Captain

---

[9] Image source:
http://www.thesun.co.uk/sol/homepage/news/1721617/Sally-Cluley-youngest-pilot-at-age-of-16.html

Chesley Sullenberger and how he saved the
passengers on his plane after it ran into a flock
of geese? During the few minutes after his
plane hit the geese, Captain Sullenberger had
to communicate with his First Officer and with
air traffic control to figure out the best way to
handle the situation. By stating clearly what
the problem was and what they needed, the
Captain and the air traffic controller were able
to consider all the options available and find
the best one. So try now to learn how to communicate clearly. The words you choose later
on as a pilot may well make the difference between a tragedy and a miracle.

Third, learn how to handle stress well. While
most flights arrive safely at their destinations
without any major problems, from time to time
an unexpected situation causes an emergency
that the pilot has to react to. If the pilot can,
despite the stress of the emergency, think
clearly and remember his or her training, then
most likely everyone will be okay. But if the pilot panics (as the first officer did on the plane
that crashed in Queens), then a small emergency can quickly turn into a catastrophe. So even
if you have an assignment due or have had a
fight with a friend or family member, make

sure you keep control of your temper and start looking for a solution.

Finally, read as much as you can about flying and about the lives of pilots. This handbook has been a great introduction, but we haven't had time to talk about the details of flying and the different types of planes. So why not go to your local flight school and ask what specialized books about flight they can recommend? Then, start reading and make sure that flying is truly the best career choice for you. If you study hard, you may discover that, like Sally Cluley in the picture you saw earlier, you may be able to get your Private Pilot Certificate while still a teenager. If your parents don't object, then why not consider taking flying lessons after you finish ground school? That way, you could be way ahead of other pilots by having hours of experience even before you go to college!

CONCLUSION

This handbook has given us a great look at what life as an airline pilot is really all about. We have seen that, while pilots have lives full of adventure and exciting destinations, they also have to learn a lot and deal with some pretty stressful situations. Let's review some of the most important things that we learned so that you don't forget them.

In the first section, we talked about what a pilot actually does and where different kinds of pilots are working today. We saw that there are military pilots, helicopter pilots, and even pilots who report on the news or traffic. But we decided to focus on airline pilots, since there are so many of them. We also saw how airline pilots may make anywhere from $20,000 to $165,000 per year, depending on their airline, experience, and position.

The second section told us what the training is like to become a pilot. We saw how pilots begin with a college education then go to ground school before taking flight lessons. Pilots focus on spending as much time in the air as possible because that is the way they measure their progress. They must take medical exams and fly alongside an instructor to make sure that they have the right qualifications to keep people safe. While they are waiting to apply to be an airline pilot, most pilots will try to work in the air some way, whether as a cargo plane pilot, a flight instructor, or in some other type of aircraft.

The third section answered the question: "Is being a pilot an easy job?" As you can probably imagine, the answer to that question is "no". Being a pilot can be a singularly stressful job day in and day out, and in this section we examined all that is required of a pilot. They are expected to be experts in many areas, including science, engineering, and legal matters. They must take all sorts of information into account when they are flying through the air, and if they stop paying attention for even a moment the results can be disastrous.

The fourth section showed us what the average day is like for an airline pilot when at work. Unlike other jobs that have a set time to start and finish, being an airline pilot means working at all kinds of strange hours for long stretches of time. Pilots begin their workday carrying out a detailed pre-flight check. Once they arrive at their destination, pilots have to wait around for anywhere from a few hours to a day or more before flying back home. During the flights, each pilot must stay alert and be ready to handle any sort of emergency that might come up.

The fifth section told us about some of the difficult moments of being a pilot. While the overall job is challenging, there are some very specific circumstances that arise every now and then that make some people decide that being a pilot is not the career for them. Pilots must deal with the rules of seniority, with no guarantee of job security, and with accepting the responsibility for hundreds of lives during each and every flight.

The sixth section told us a little about what the future is for the career of a pilot. In ten years or so, right about the time that you may decide whether or not being a pilot is the right career for you there will be some exciting opportunities for pilots. While there may be fewer airlines and fewer flights, new technology might make planes look terribly different. Future airline pilots may even go into space!

Finally, the seventh section told you what you can do right now to get ready to become an airline pilot. Although most airline pilots must have a college education before they can get hired to fly, there are certain qualities and skills that you can develop right now to help you reach your goals more quickly. We saw how developing a love for math and science, learning to communicate well, learning how to handle stress, and reading can all help you to reach your goal of being an airline pilot.

The career of a pilot is one of most exciting jobs that you can imagine. If you think that you can deal with some of the tough conditions that come with being a pilot, then you can be sure that you will never get tired of flying through the air and looking down at the world from high above.

Pilots are the happiest when they are in the air[10]

---

[10] Image source:
http://greatarcticairadventure.com/blog1/category/jim/

Lightning Source UK Ltd.
Milton Keynes UK
UKHW010801310520
364102UK00003B/729